ONE MINUTE
NONSENSE

ANTHONY DE MELLO, S.J.

ONE MINUTE
NONSENSE

Loyola Press

Chicago

©1992 Gujarat Sahitya Prakash, Anand, India
Original English edition

Loyola Press
3441 North Ashland Avenue
Chicago, Illinois 60657

Library of Congress Cataloging-in-Publication Data
De Mello, Anthony, 1931- 87
    One minute nonsense/by Anthony de Mello.—
U.S. and Canadian ed.
          p.   cm.
    ISBN 0-8294-0742-1 (pbk.)
    1. Meditations.   I. Title.
    BX2182.2.D3875   1992
    242—dc20   92-31735
                                               CIP

Cover and interior design by Nancy Gruenke.
The cover was adapted from the cover for *Contact with God:
Retreat Conferences* (Anthony de Mello, S.J. [Chicago: Loyola
University Press, 1991]) by Beth Herman Design Associates.

01 00 99 98 97   5 4 3 2 1

A NOTE FROM THE AMERICAN PUBLISHER

Tony de Mello's last posthumous publication, *One Minute Nonsense,* was originally published in India as a one-volume edition. Loyola University Press has chosen to make it available as two books, including the present volume, *One Minute Nonsense,* and a volume to come, *More One Minute Nonsense.* This is partly to stretch out, if we could, our leave-taking of a contemporary author whose spirit, stories, and imagery profoundly enriched the terms of spiritual reflection today.

Father X. Diaz del Rio, S.J., director of Gujarat Sahitya Prakash, the original publisher of *One Minute Nonsense* (1992), did a favor to all the readers and lovers of Father de Mello's work when he wrote the following preface, taking us through some of the last days of this remarkable mentor:

> We are bringing out the last posthumous book of Tony de Mello, *One Minute Nonsense.*
>
> Actually he wrote it after *One Minute Wisdom* and before *The Prayer of the*

Frog. He sent the manuscript to the
publisher with instructions to print
it soon. It was as it appears now: the
stories had no titles and there was no
table of contents. The text was typed,
except the short commentary to the first
story that was handwritten by him.
The typesetting was about to start when
at the end of 1986 he wrote again:
"I am writing another book, which will
be entitled *The Prayer of the Frog,* and
it has to appear before *One Minute
Nonsense;* please send the manuscript
back to me."

In the early months of 1987 Tony
worked hard on *The Prayer of the Frog.*
He wanted to hand over the manuscript
for publication before his departure for
New York at the end of May. I met Tony
in Bombay on May 30. We discussed
the layout of the book for several hours.
After completing that work I asked
Tony about the manuscript of *One
Minute Nonsense.* He told me that it
was ready and he would send it to
me immediately on his return from
America. After that he would start
preparing a book of meditations.

At about six o'clock that evening
I wished Tony goodbye and left to catch
my train back to Gujarat. Two hours
later he himself left for the airport.
He died at Fordham University, the
very night of his first day in New York,
June 1, 1987.

He never expected to be back so
soon. His body arrived in the morning
of June 13 and was buried the same
evening in the cemetery at St. Peter's
Church, Bandra, where he had been
baptized.

Among his papers . . . *One Minute
Nonsense* [was found]. "Ready for the
press" he had said, but the stories had
no title and there was no table of
contents. Did he intend to add them?
We shall never know; but probably not,
since he told me "it is ready for the
press."

And so we are bringing out his last
book, *One Minute Nonsense,* the one he
wanted to come after *The Prayer of the
Frog.* We publish it as he left it, without
titles and without contents, just the

stories, one after the other, in the same
order in which he left them.

Our thanks to Father del Rio, not only as the
original publisher of a number of Father de
Mello's books but for the personal report above.
Father de Mello was not only the complete
professional. He inspired friendship broadly
and tears from many when the Lord took him
home on short notice.

Rev. Joseph F. Downey, S.J.
Editorial Director
Loyola University Press

"The man talks nonsense," said a visitor after hearing the Master speak.

Said a disciple, "You would talk nonsense too if you were trying to express the Inexpressible."

> While the visitor checked this out with the Master himself, this is the reply he got: "No one is exempt from talking nonsense. The great misfortune is to do it solemnly."

From the manuscript handwritten by Fr. de Mello

The Master in these tales is not a single person. He is a Hindu guru, a Zen roshi, a Taoist sage, a Jewish rabbi, a Christian monk, a Sufi mystic. He is Lao Tzu and Socrates, Buddha and Jesus, Zarathustra and Mohammed. His teaching is found in the seventh century B.C. and the twentieth century A.D. His wisdom belongs to East and West alike. Do his historical antecedents really matter? History, after all, is the record of appearances, not Reality; of doctrines, not of Silence.

It will only take a minute to read each of the
anecdotes that follow. You will probably find
the Master's language baffling, exasperating,
even downright meaningless. This, alas, is not
an easy book! It was written, not to instruct, but
to Awaken. Concealed within its pages (not in
the printed words, not even in the tales, but in
its spirit, its mood, its atmosphere) is a Wisdom
that cannot be conveyed in human speech. As
you read the printed page and struggle within
the Master's cryptic language it is possible that
you will unwittingly chance upon the Silent
Teaching that lurks within the book, and be
Awakened—and transformed. This is what
Wisdom means: To be changed without the
slightest effort on your part, to be transformed,
believe it or not, merely by waking to the reality
that is not words, that lies beyond the reach
of words.

If you are fortunate enough to be Awakened
thus, you will know why the finest language
is the one that is not spoken, the finest action
is the one that is not done, and the finest change
is the one that is not willed.

Caution: Take the tales in tiny doses—one
or two at a time. An overdose will lower their
potency.

ONE MINUTE NONSENSE

Said a disciple to a newcomer at the monastery, "I must warn you that you will not understand a word of what the Master says if you do not have the proper disposition."

"What is the proper disposition?"

"Be like a student eager to learn a foreign language. The words he speaks sound familiar, but don't be taken in; they have an altogether foreign meaning."

The Master could be quite critical when he
thought that criticism was in order.

But to everyone's surprise he was never
resented for his reprimands. When asked
about this once, he said, "It depends on how
one does it. Human beings are flowers: open
and receptive to softly falling dew, closed to
violent rain."

"A good way to discover your shortcomings," said the Master, "is to observe what irritates you in others."

He once told how his wife had placed a candy box on the kitchen shelf only to find, an hour later, that the box felt light. The whole bottom layer was gone, each piece neatly dropped into a paper bag that sat atop the new cook's belongings. Not willing to cause embarrassment, the kind-hearted woman merely replaced the candy and kept it in a cupboard out of temptation's way.

After dinner the cook announced she was leaving the job—that very night.

"Why? What's the matter?" asked the Master.

"I won't work for people who steal back," was her defiant reply.

Next day the Master followed this up with the story of the burglar who found this sign on the door of the safe he was about to blow: "Please do not use dynamite. This safe is not locked. Just turn the knob."

The instant he turned the knob a sand bag fell on him, the premises were flood-lit and sirens woke the entire neighborhood.

When the Master visited the man in prison he found him bitter: "How am I ever going to trust another human being again?"

When a guest volunteered to do the dishes after
dinner the Master said, "Are you sure you know
how to do dishes?"

The man protested that he had done them all his
life. Said the Master: "Ah, I have no doubt of
your ability to make dishes clean—I only doubt
your ability to wash them."

This is the explanation he gave his disciples
later: "There are two ways to wash dishes: one
is to wash them in order to make them clean;
the other is to wash them in order to wash
them."

That was still far from clear, so he added: "The
first action is dead because while your body
does the dishes your mind is fixed on the goal
of cleaning them; the second is alive because
your mind is where your body is."

"Enlightenment," said the Master, "means knowing precisely where you are at any given moment—not an easy task at all!"

And he told of a popular friend of his who was, even in his late eighties, invited to dozens of functions. Once he was spotted at a party and asked how many he was attending that night.

"Six," said the elderly gentleman, without taking his eyes off his little notebook.

"What are you doing? Seeing where you are to go next?" they asked him.

"No," said the dynamic fellow. "Finding out where I am now."

The Master was allergic to ideologies.

"In a war of ideas," he said, "it is people who are the casualties."

Later he elaborated: "People kill for money or for power. But the most ruthless murderers are those who kill for their ideas."

It was lecture time and the Master said, "The genius of a composer is found in the notes of his music—but analyzing the notes will not reveal his genius. The poet's greatness is contained in his words—yet the study of his words will not disclose his inspiration. God reveals himself in creation—but scrutinize creation as minutely as you wish, you will not find God, any more than you will find the soul through the careful examination of your body."

At question time someone asked, "How then shall we find God?"

"By looking at creation, not by analyzing it."

"And how is one to look?"

"A peasant sets out to find beauty in the sunset, but all he finds is sun and cloud and sky and earth's horizon—till he understands that beauty is not a 'thing' but a special way of looking. You will seek for God in vain till you understand that God can't be seen as 'thing'; he needs a special way of looking—similar to that of little children whose sight is undistorted by prefabricated doctrines and beliefs."

The father of one of the disciples stormed into the lecture hall where the Master was holding forth.

Ignoring everyone present he yelled at his daughter, "You have abandoned a university career to sit at the feet of this fool! What has he taught you?"

She stood up, calmly drew her father outside, and said, "Being with him has taught me what no university ever could—not to fear you and not to be embarrassed by your disgraceful behavior."

"What does one need in order to be
enlightened?" asked the disciples.

Said the Master, "You must discover what
it is that falls in the water and does not make
a ripple; moves through the trees and does not
make a sound; enters the field and does not stir
a single blade of grass."

After weeks of fruitless pondering, the disciples
said, "What is this thing?"

"Thing?" said the Master. "But it isn't a thing
at all."

"So it is nothing?"

"You might say so."

"Then how are we to search for it?"

"Did I tell you to search for it? It can be found
but never searched for. Seek and you will miss."

The Master overheard an actress discoursing on horoscopes at dinner time.

He leaned over and said, "You don't believe in astrology, do you?"

"Well," she replied, "I believe in everything a little bit."

Someone asked the Master if he believed in luck.

"Certainly," he replied with a twinkle in his eye. "How else can one explain the success of people one does not like?"

The Master was unsparing of those who wallowed in self-pity or resentment.

"To be wronged," he said, "is *nothing* unless you insist on remembering it."

The Master once told of a woman who complained to the police that she had been raped.

"Describe the man," said the officer.

"Well, to begin with he was an *idiot!*"

"An idiot, ma'am?"

"Yes. He didn't know a thing and I had to help him!"

That sounded less funny when the Master added: "Any time you take offense find out how you helped the offender."

This raised a storm of protest, so he added, "Can anyone offend you if you refuse to take offense?"

When asked how Scripture is to be used the
Master told of the time he was a school teacher
and set the students this question: "How would
you determine the height of a building by
means of an aneroid barometer?"

One bright young fellow replied, "I would
lower the barometer on a string and measure
the string."

"Resourceful in his ignorance," was the Master's
comment.

Then he added: "Such is the resourcefulness
and the ignorance of those who use their brain
to understand Scripture which can as well be
'understood' by the brain as can a sunset or the
ocean or the murmur of the night wind in the
trees."

"People don't want to give up their jealousies
and anxieties, their resentment and guilt,
because these negative emotions provide them
with their 'kicks,' the feeling of being alive,"
said the Master.

And this is how he illustrated it:

The local postman took a short cut through a
meadow on his bicycle. Midway across, a bull
spied him and gave chase. The poor fellow
barely made it to the fence.

"Nearly got you, didn't he?" said the Master who
had watched the scene.

"Yes," said the old man, puffing, "nearly gets me
every time."

A scientist came to protest that the Master's contempt for concepts as opposed to "conceptless-knowledge" was unfair to science.

The Master was at pains to explain that he was a friend of science. "But," he said, "your knowledge of your wife had better go beyond the concept-knowledge of science!"

Later, when talking to his disciples, he was even more forceful. "Concepts define," he said. "To define is to destroy. Concepts dissect Reality. And what you dissect you kill."

"Are concepts then quite useless?"

"No. Dissect a rose and you will have valuable information—and no knowledge whatsoever— of the rose. Become a scholar and you will have much information—but no knowledge whatsoever—of Reality."

The Master claimed that the world most people see is not the world of Reality, but a world their head creates.

When a scholar came to dispute this, the Master set two sticks on the floor in the form of the letter *T* and asked, "What do you see here?"

"The letter *T*," said the scholar.

"Just as I thought," said the Master. "There's no such things as a letter *T*; that's a symbol in your head. What you have here is two broken branches in the form of sticks."

"When you speak about Reality," said the Master, "you are attempting to put the Inexpressible into words, so your words are certain to be misunderstood. Thus people who read that expression of Reality called the Scriptures become stupid and cruel for they follow, not their common sense, but what they think their Scriptures say." He had the perfect parable to show this:

> A village blacksmith found an apprentice willing to work hard at low pay. The smith immediately began his instructions to the lad: "When I take the metal out of the fire, I'll lay it on the anvil; and when I nod my head you hit it with the hammer." The apprentice did precisely what *he* *thought* he was told. Next day he was the village blacksmith.

To a disciple who was terrified about making mistakes, the Master said:

"Those who make no mistakes are making the biggest mistake of all—they are attempting nothing new."

"Tell me," said the atheist. "Is there a God—
really?"

Said the Master, "If you want me to be perfectly
honest with you, I will not answer."

Later the disciples demanded to know why he
had not answered.

"Because his question is unanswerable," said
the Master.

"So you are an atheist?"

"Certainly not. The atheist makes the mistake
of denying that of which nothing may be said."

After pausing to let that sink in, he added, "And
the theist makes the mistake of affirming it."

"What is the secret of your serenity?"

Said the Master, "Wholehearted cooperation with the inevitable."

The Master and a disciple came upon a blind man sitting on the sidewalk, begging.

Said the Master, "Give the man an alms."

The disciple dropped a coin in the beggar's hat.

Said the Master, "You should have touched your hat as a mark of respect."

"Why?" asked the disciple.

"One always should when one gives an alms."

"But the man was blind."

"You never know," said the Master. "He may have been a fraud."

The monastery was getting crowded and a
larger building was needed, so a merchant
wrote out a check for a million dollars and
placed it before the Master who picked it up
and said, "Very well. I shall accept it."

The merchant was dissatisfied. That was a large
sum of money and the Master hadn't even
thanked him.

"There are a million dollars in that check,"
he said.

"Yes, so I have observed."

"Even if I am a wealthy man, a million dollars
is a lot of money."

"Do you want me to thank you for it?"

"You ought to."

"Why should I? The giver should be thankful,"
said the Master.

The Master's attitude to social service was
perplexing. At times he was all for it. At others
he seemed indifferent.

The explanations he sometimes gave for this
inconsistency were just as enigmatic. He said:

"The one who wishes to do good must knock
at the gate.

"For the one who loves, the gate is always
open."

Said the tourist, "The people of your country are poor. But they never seem preoccupied."

Said the Master, "That is because they never look at the clock."

A disciple had to rush back home when he got news that his house had burned down.

He was an old man and everyone commiserated with him on his return. All that the Master said to him was, "This will make dying easier."

The Enlightened person, said the Master, is one who sees that everything in the world is perfect exactly as it is.

"What about the gardener?" someone asked. "Is he perfect too?"

The monastery gardener was a hunchback.

"For what he is meant to be in life," said the Master, "the gardener is a perfect hunchback."

The idea that everything in the world is perfect was more than the disciples could accept. So the Master put it in concepts that were more within their grasp. "God weaves perfect designs with the threads of our lives," he said, "even with our sins. The reason we can't see this is we're looking at the reverse side of the tapestry."

And, more succinctly, "What some people take for a shiny stone the jeweler recognizes as a diamond."

The disciples were distressed to see the
Master's teachings ridiculed in a national
magazine.

The Master was unperturbed. "Could anything
be really true," he said, "if no one laughed at it?"

In his younger days the Master had been a political activist and had led a protest march against the government. Thousands of people had left their homes and jobs to join the agitation.

The march had hardly begun when he called the whole thing off. "You simply cannot do this; this march has been planned for months and has cost the people dearly. They will accuse you of being inconsistent," said his agitated followers.

The Master was unmoved. "My commitment is not to consistency," he said, "but to the Truth."

The Master taught that one reason people are so unhappy is that they think there is nothing that they cannot change.

He especially enjoyed the story of the man who says to the shopkeeper, "This radio you sold me is excellent for quality of sound; but I want it exchanged for one that has better programs."

"What is it you seek?"

"Peace," said the visitor.

"To those who seek to protect their ego true
Peace only brings disturbance."

And to a religious group that came to gawk
at him and ask for a blessing, he said with a
roguish smile, "May the peace of God disturb
you always!"

Back from a journey the Master told of an
experience he thought was a parable on life:

During a brief stop he walked to a neat-looking
lunch counter. There were delicious soups and
hot curries and all sorts of tempting dishes.

He ordered a soup.

"Are you from the bus?" a matronly attendant
asked. The Master nodded.

"No soup."

"Hot curry with steamed rice?" asked the Master,
puzzled.

"Not if you're on the bus. You can have
sandwiches. It took me all morning to prepare
that food and you have no more than ten
minutes to eat it. I won't let you eat food that
you don't have the time to relish."

There was nothing pompous about the Master.
Wild, hilarious laughter prevailed each time he
spoke, to the dismay of those who were solemn
about their spirituality—and themselves.

Said one disillusioned visitor, "The man's a
clown!"

"No, no," said a disciple. "You've missed the
point: a clown gets you to laugh at him, a
Master gets you to laugh at yourself."

"How does one learn to trust in Providence?"

"Trust in Providence," said the Master, "is like walking into an expensive restaurant without a cent in your pocket and eating dozens of oysters in the hope of finding a pearl to pay the bill!"

It scandalized the disciples that the Master had such little use for worship.

"Find yourself an object of veneration," he used to say, "and you piously distract yourself from what is essential—awareness that leads to love."

And in self-defense he would cite Jesus' scorn of those who cried, "Lord, Lord," and were quite unaware of the evil they were doing.

He once offered a banana to an awe-stricken visitor who so venerated the gift that he hardly knew what to do with it.

When the Master was told of this he said characteristically, "Tell the silly ass to eat it."

Said a recently arrived disciple to one with
more experience, "Why do I seem to gain
so little from living with the Master?"

"Could it be because you came to learn
spirituality from him?"

"What, may I ask, did you come for?"

"To see him fasten his sandal straps!"

It was a joy to behold the Master perform the
simplest acts—sit or walk or drink a cup of tea
or drive away a fly. There was a grace in all
he did that made him seem in harmony with
Nature, as though his actions were produced
not by him, but by the Universe.

Once when he received a parcel the disciples,
spellbound, watched him reverently untie the
string, unfold the paper, and lift the contents
as though the parcel were a living creature.

A religious woman told the Master she had
been to confession that morning.

"I can't imagine you committing a grave sin,"
said the Master. "What did you confess?"

"Well, I was too lazy to go to Mass one Sunday,
and I swore at the gardener once. And I once
drove my mother-in-law out of the house for
a whole week."

"But that happened five years ago, didn't it?
Surely you've been to confession since then."

"Yes, I have. But I confess it every time. I just
like to remember it."

"Some day you will understand that you are seeking what you already have," said the Master to an intense disciple.

"Then why do I not see it now?"

"Because you are trying to."

"Must I then make no efforts?"

"If you relax and give it time, it will make itself known."

For people who practiced virtue in order to get God's friendship or favor, the Master had this to say:

A large crowd of people were taking part in a Cadillac giveaway contest sponsored by a soap manufacturer.

They were asked, "Why do you like Heaven Scent Soap?"

One woman's honest reply was, "Because I'd love to own a Cadillac."

"I have been four months with you and you have still given me no method or technique."

"A method?" said the Master. "What on earth would you want a method for?"

"To attain to inner freedom."

The Master roared with laughter. "You need great skill indeed to set yourself free by means of the trap called a method," he said.

When a disciple complained that the Master's
spirituality needed updating the Master laughed
aloud. Then he told the story of a student who
said, "Haven't you any more recent books on
anatomy? These are at least ten years old."

Said the bookseller, "Look, son, there have
been no bones added to the human body in the
last ten years."

"Neither," added the Master, "has there been
any addition to human nature in the last ten
thousand years."

The Master once proposed a riddle: "What do the artist and the musician have in common with the mystic?"

Everyone gave up.

"The realization that the finest speech does not come from the tongue," said the Master.

The Master was walking down a street when a man rushed out of a doorway and the two collided with great force.

The man was beside himself with rage and exploded into abusive language. The Master made a little bow, smiled pleasantly, and said, "My friend, I do not know which of us is responsible for this encounter, but I am not inclined to waste time investigating. If I ran into you, I beg your pardon; if you ran into me, don't mention it."

Then, with another smile and bow he walked away.

To a painter the Master said: "To be successful, every painter must invest hours in unremitting toil and effort.

"To some it will be given to let go of the ego as they paint. When this happens, a masterpiece is born."

Later, a disciple asked, "Who is a Master?"

The Master replied, "Anyone to whom it is given to let go of the ego. Such a person's life is then a masterpiece."

The Master always taught that Truth was right
before our eyes and the reason we did not see
it was our lack of perspective.

Once he took a disciple on a mountain trip.
When they were halfway up the mountain the
man glared at the underbrush and complained,
"Where's the beautiful scenery you are always
talking about?"

The Master grinned. "You're standing on top
of it as you will see when we reach the peak."

"Where shall I find a worthy Master when I get back to my country?"

"There isn't a single moment when you are without one."

The disciple was confused.

"Simply watching your reaction to everything— a bird, a leaf, a tear, a smile—makes everything your Master."

The Master was certainly not a stickler for etiquette and good manners but there was always a natural courtesy and grace in his dealings with others.

A young disciple was once very rude to a traffic policeman as he drove the Master home one night. In self-defense he said, "I'd rather be myself and let people know exactly how I feel. Politeness is nothing but a lot of hot air."

"True enough," said the Master pleasantly, "but that's what we have in our automobile tires and see how it eases the bumps."

Rarely was the Master so eloquent as when he
warned against the bewitching power of words:

"Beware of the words," he said, "the moment
you look away they will take on a life of their
own; they will dazzle, mesmerize, terrorize—
lead you astray from the reality they
represent—lead you to believe they are real.

"The world you see is not the Kingdom seen by
children but a fragmented world, broken into a
thousand pieces by the word . . . It is as if each
ocean wave were seen to be distinct and
separate from the body of the ocean.

"When words and thoughts are silenced the
Universe blossoms forth—real and whole and
one—and words become what they were always
meant to be: the score, not the music; the menu,
not the food; the signpost, not journey's end."

Once when the Master spoke of the hypnotic power of words someone from the back of the room shouted, "You're talking nonsense! If I say, 'God, God, God,' will that make me divine? And if I say, 'Sin, Sin, Sin,' will it make me evil?"

"Sit down, you bastard!" said the Master.

The man became so livid with rage it took him some time to recover his speech. Then he screamed a torrent of abuse at the Master.

The Master, looking contrite, said, "Pardon me, sir, I was carried away. I truly apologize for my unpardonable lapse."

The man calmed down immediately.

"Well, there you have your answer: all it took was a word to give you a fit and another to sedate you," said the Master.

The governor resigned his exalted office and came to the Master demanding to be taught.

"What is it you wish me to teach you?" said the Master.

"Wisdom," was the reply.

"Ah, my friend! How gladly would I do that were it not for one major obstacle."

"What?"

"Wisdom can't be taught."

"So there's nothing I can learn here."

"Wisdom can be learned. But it can't be taught."

Some of the disciples were on an excursion
high up on a snow-clad mountain. Everywhere
a cosmic silence prevailed. They were curious
to find out if there were any sounds at night so
they pressed a record button on a tape recorder,
left it at the entrance of their tent, and went to
sleep.

They got back to the monastery and replayed
the tape. Not a sound; total, unsullied silence.

The Master, who was listening to the tape,
broke in with: "Don't you hear it?"

"Hear what?"

"The harmony of galaxies in motion," said the
Master.

The disciples looked at one another in wonder.

Attachment distorts our perception—this was
a frequent theme of the Master's discourses.

The disciples were once entertained to a perfect
example of this when they heard the Master ask
a mother, "How is your daughter?"

"My darling daughter! How fortunate she is! She
has such a wonderful husband! He has given
her a car, all the jewelery she wants, servants
galore. He serves her breakfast in bed, and she
doesn't get up till noon. What a prince of a
man!"

"And your son?"

"Oh the poor boy! What a vixen he has married!
He has given a car, all the jewelery she wants,
and an army of servants. And she stays in bed
till noon! Won't even get up to give him his
breakfast!"

Everyone was talking about the religious man
who lost his life in a suicide attack.

While no one in the monastery approved of the
man's action, some said they admired his faith.

"Faith?" said the Master.

"Well, he had the courage of his convictions,
didn't he?"

"That was fanaticism, not faith. Faith demands
a greater courage still: to reexamine one's
convictions and reject them if they do not fit the
facts."

When the Master was a boy at school, a
classmate treated him with persistent cruelty.

Now, older and contrite, he came to the
monastery and was received with open arms.

One day he brought up the subject of his former
cruelty, but the Master seemed not to recall it.

Said the visitor, "Don't you remember?"

Said the Master, "I distinctly remember
forgetting it!" so they both melted in innocent
laughter.

A mother asked when she should begin the education of her child.

"How old is she?" asked the Master.

"She's five."

"Five! Hurry home! You're five years late already."

When the Master heard that a neighboring
forest had been devastated by fire, he mobilized
all his disciples. "We must replant the cedars,"
he said.

"The cedars?" exclaimed an incredulous
disciple. "But they take two thousand years
to grow!"

"In that case," said the Master, "there's not
a minute to lose. We must set out at once."

A friend said to a university student, "What do you go to the Master for? Will he help you earn a living?"

"No, but thanks to him I will know what to do with the living when I earn one," was the reply.

"Your religious leaders are just as blind and confused as you are," said the Master. "When confronted with life's problems all they come up with is answers from a Book. But Life is too large to fit into any book."

To illustrate this he told of the thug who said, "This is a holdup! Give me your money or else."

"Or else what?"

"Don't confuse me. This is my first job."

"How does the Master explain the evil in the world?" asked a visitor.

One disciple replied, "He doesn't explain it. He's too busy doing something about it."

Said another, "People are forever fighting the world or bored with it. The Master is enchanted with what he sees as stupendous, awesome, unfathomable."

The preacher was widely acclaimed for his eloquence. But he confessed to his friends that his eloquent speech never had quite the effect of the Master's unadorned pronouncements.

After living with the Master for a week he knew exactly why.

"When he speaks," said the preacher, "his speech embodies silence. My speech, alas, embodies thought."

The Master had what amounted to a veneration for the human body. When a disciple referred to it as an "earthern vessel" the Master rapturously quoted the poet Kabir:

"Within this earthern vessel are canyons and Himalayan mountains; the seven seas are here and a thousand million galaxies; and the music of the spheres and the source of waterfalls and rivers."

When the Master met a group of teachers he spoke long and animatedly for he had been a teacher himself. The trouble with teachers, he said, is that they keep forgetting that the goal of education is not learning but life.

He told of the time he spotted a boy fishing in the river.

"Hello! Nice day for fishing!" he said to the youngster.

"Yes," came the reply.

After a while the Master said, "Why aren't you in school today?"

"Well, sir, like you said—it's a nice day for fishing."

And he told of the report card his little daughter got: "Meena is doing well in school. She would do much better if the pure joy of living did not impede her progress."

The Master loved to show how nature is shot through with holiness. He was once sitting in the garden when he exclaimed:

"Look at that bright blue bird sitting on the branch of that tree springing up and down, up and down, filling the world with its melody, abandoning itself to unreserved delight because it has no notion of tomorrow."

"The law is an expression of God's holy will and as such must be honored and loved," said the preacher piously.

"Rubbish," said the Master. "The law is a necessary evil and as such must be cut down to the barest minimum. Show me a lover of the law and I will show you a muttonheaded tyrant."

He once told of his sister who got tired of pushing her daughter's baby carriage, so she had a motor put on it. Then the police stepped into the picture. First they said the powered carriage could travel three miles an hour so it had to be classified as a "self-propelled vehicle." Therefore the mother would have to get a license, plates, lights, and brakes; and, to crown it all, a driver's license!

The Master went on to tell of the astronaut who
returned from a five-hundred-orbit voyage
round the earth. When asked how he felt, he
said, "Exhausted! Think how many times I had
to say the morning, noon, evening, and night
prayers prescribed by my religion!"

For the Master all rules, no matter how sacred, had a purely functional value, and had to yield to Reality, which alone was Law Supreme.

When his teenage daughter, following the fashion, wanted to wear an off-the-shoulder dress, her mother felt she wasn't old enough for that sort of gown. A heated argument ensued— for days.

When the Master was finally appealed to, he said, "Let her try one on. If it stays up—she's old enough to wear it."

The man was a religious writer and asked for
a word of wisdom. Said the Master:

"Some people write to make a living; others to
share their insights or raise questions that will
haunt their readers; others yet to understand
their very souls.

"None of these will last. That distinction belongs
to those who write only because if they did not
they would burst."

As an afterthought he added: "These writers
give expression to the divine—no matter *what*
they write about."

When asked what enlightenment felt like, the Master said, "It is like going into the wilderness and suddenly feeling that you are being watched."

"By whom?"

"By rocks and trees and mountains."

"An eerie feeling."

"No, a comforting one. But because it is unfamiliar one feels the urge to rush back to the commonplace world of people—their noise, their words, their laughter—which has cut us off from Nature and Reality."

When asked if he was never discouraged by the little fruit his efforts seemed to yield, the Master told the story of a snail that started to climb a cherry tree one cold, windy day in late spring.

The sparrows on a neighboring tree had a good laugh at his expense. Then one flew over and said, "Hey, blockhead, don't you know there are no cherries on this tree?"

The little fellow did not stop as he replied, "Well, there will be when I get there."

A disciple was prone to fits of prolonged depression. "My doctor insists I take medication to keep my depression at bay," he said.

"Well, then, why don't you?" said the Master.

"Because it might damage my liver and shorten my life."

Said the Master, "Would you rather have a healthy liver than a happy mood? One year of life is worth more than twenty years of hibernation."

Later he said to his disciples: "It is with life as with a tale; not how long it is but how good, is what matters."

One day the Master said, "Good deeds done by the unconscious are superior to those that are willed."

This produced a flurry of questions that the Master nimbly side-stepped as he always did when he judged that the time to answer them had not arrived.

One day everyone went to the performance of a world-famous pianist. Said the Master in a whisper to his neighbor, "The movement of that woman's fingers over the keyboard is something that cannot be willed. Work of that quality must be left to the unconscious."

"Does it ever bring you joy to see the fruits of
your endeavors?"

"How much joy does it give a tool to see what
the hand has done?"

A visitor to the monastery was particularly
struck by what he called the Master's radiance.
One day when he happened to meet an old
friend of the Master's, he asked if there was
any explanation for it.

Said the friend, "Let me put it this way: Life is
a Mystery. Death is the key that unlocks it. The
moment you turn the key you disappear into the
Mystery forever."

"Do we have to wait for death before we turn the
key?" said the visitor.

"No! You could turn it now—through Silence—
and dissolve into the Mystery. Then you too
would become radiant—like the Master."

Someone asked the Master the meaning of a phrase he had heard: "The enlightened person travels without moving."

Said the Master: "Sit at your window each day and observe the ever-changing scenery in your backyard as the earth carries you through its annual trip round the sun."

Enthralled at hearing the Master chant Sanskrit verses in a melodious voice, a Sanskrit scholar said, "I have always known that there is no language on earth like Sanskrit for the expression of things divine."

"Don't be an ass," said the Master. "The language of the divine isn't Sanskrit. It is Silence."

The Master was amused at the kind of phony self-deprecation that passes for humility. Here is a parable he told his disciples:

> Two men went to a church to pray, a priest and a sexton. The priest began to beat his breast and, carried away, cried out, "I am the lowliest of men, Lord, unworthy of your grace! I am a void, a nothing—have mercy on me."
>
> Not far from the priest was the sexton who, in an outburst of fervor, also beat his breast and cried, "Have mercy, Lord! I'm a sinner, a nothing."
>
> The priest turned round haughtily. "Ha!" he said. "Look who's claiming to be nothing!"

"Name one practical, down-to-earth effect of spirituality," said the skeptic who was ready for an argument.

"Here's one," said the Master. "When someone offends you, you can raise your spirits to heights where offenses cannot reach."

"Why . . . why . . . why?" demanded the disciple when, to his astonishment, the Master insisted on his leaving the monastery forthwith barely twenty-four hours after he had been welcomed.

"Because you do not need a Master. I can show you the way, but only you can do the walking. I can point to the water, you alone can do the drinking. Why waste your time here gazing starry-eyed at me? You know the way. Walk! The water is right in front of you. Drink!"

A group of pilgrims decided to include a visit to the Master in their itinerary. When they were in his presence they asked for a word of religious wisdom.

The Master, who was quick to spot people in the religion business, said, "Understand that you are not truly spiritual at all."

Not one bit pleased at this offense to their ego, they demanded an explanation. Said the Master:

> A rabbit and a lion once walked into a restaurant.
>
> Everyone in the restaurant stopped to look. They couldn't believe what they were seeing.
>
> Said the rabbit to the waiter, "Lettuce, please—no dressing."
>
> "What about your friend," said the waiter. "What shall I bring him?"
>
> "Nothing."
>
> "You mean the lion isn't hungry?"
>
> The rabbit looked the waiter in the eye and said, "If he were a lion, do you think he would be sitting here? He's a sham!"

Said a curious disciple, "Give us a sign to know when one is enlightened."

Said the Master, "Here's one. You find yourself asking, 'Is it I who am crazy, or is it everyone else?'"

In respect of preachers and priests the Master always urged people to look for competence not claims.

Two tourists were approaching Honolulu, he said, and got into an argument about the correct pronunciation of Hawaii. One said it was "Hawaii," the other affirmed it was "Havaii."

The first thing they did on landing was approach a native. "Aloha! How do you people pronounce the name of the island: 'Hawaii' or 'Havaii'?"

"Havaii," said the native.

"Thank you."

"A very varm velcome to both of you," said the native.

"What is the work of a Master?" said a solemn-faced visitor.

"To teach people to laugh," said the Master gravely.

Another time he declared:

"When you are able to laugh in the face of life
you become sovereign of the world—just like
the person who is prepared to die."

"How does one recognize enlightenment?"

"By the fact that, having seen evil as evil, the
enlightened person cannot do it," said the
Master.

And he added, "And cannot be tempted either.
All the others are frauds."

Then he told the story of a smuggler who,
fearing police raids, went to a very holy monk
to beg him to hide some contraband goods in
his monastery for, given his reputation for
holiness, no one would suspect him.

The monk drew himself up indignantly and
demanded that the man leave the monastery
at once.

"I'll give you a hundred thousand dollars for
your charities," said the smuggler.

The monk hesitated, ever so slightly, before
saying no.

"Two hundred thousand." Still the monk refused.

"Five hundred thousand." The monk took hold
of a stick and yelled, "Get out this minute.
You're getting too close to my price."

"Only a foolish person would hesitate to give up everything in exchange for Truth," said the Master.

And he told them the following parable:

During an oil boom in a small country town landowners eagerly sold every square foot of land to the oil companies in exchange for fortunes.

One old lady refused to sell at any price.

The offers rose to astronomical figures till one oil company declared it was ready to give her any price she named. Still she held out, so an agitated friend demanded to know why. Said the old lady, "Don't you see that if I sell, I'll lose my only source of income."

"I am affluent, but miserable. Why?"

"Because you spend too much time making money and too little making love," said the Master.

The Master taught that change, even change for
the good, always carried side effects that had to
be carefully examined before the change was
sought: the invention of gunpowder brought
protection from wild beasts—and modern
warfare. The automobile brought speed—and
air pollution. Modern technology saves lives—
and makes our bodies flabby.

"There was once a man," he said, "who had
a golden belly button that caused him endless
embarrassment for each time he took a shower
or swim he was the butt of people's jokes.
He prayed and prayed to have the belly button
changed—then one night he dreamt that an
angel unscrewed it and, leaving it on a table,
disappeared. On awaking in the morning he saw
the dream was true—there on the table lay the
shiny golden belly button. The man jumped up
in ecstasy—and his real belly button fell off!"

A philosopher asked, "What is the purpose of creation?"

"Lovemaking," said the Master.

Later, to his disciples, he said, "Before creation love was. After creation love is made. When love is consummated, creation will cease to be, and love will be forever."

One day when the talk turned to modern technology the Master told of a friend of his who wanted to encourage a taste for music in his children. So he bought them a piano.

When he got home that evening he found them contemplating the piano in puzzlement. "How," they asked, "do you plug it in?"

When he was a young man the Master had done
a lot of traveling around the world. He was at
the port of Shanghai, China, once when he
heard loud screaming next to his boat. Looking
out, he saw a man leaning over the side of a
nearby junk hanging on to the pigtail of another
man who was thrashing about in the water.

The man in the junk would push the other under
the water, then yank him up again. The two
would then argue wildly for a minute or so
before the dunking was repeated.

The Master rang for the cabin boy and asked
what the quarrel was about. The boy listened
for a moment, laughed, and said, "Nothing, sir.
Man in boat want sixty yuan to not drown other
man. Man in water say no, only forty yuan."

After the disciples laughed at the story the
master said, "Is there a single one of you who
isn't bargaining about the only Life there is?"
All of them were silent.

"Who is a happy person?"

"One who has no resources and no hopes—and doesn't desire any," said the Master.

The Master never let a statement about God go unchallenged. All God statements were poetic or symbolical expressions of the Unknowable; people, however, foolishly took them as literal descriptions of the divine.

When the preacher said, "This much I know of God, that he is wise and good," the Master countered with, "Then why does he stand by helplessly in the face of evil?"

Said the preacher, "How should I know? What do you think I am, a mystic?"

Later the Master regaled his disciples with this Jewish tale:

> Two men sat sipping tea in silence. After a while one said, "Life is like a bowl of lukewarm soup."
>
> "Like a bowl of lukewarm soup?" asked the other. "Why?"
>
> "How should I know? What do you think I am, a philosopher?"

The Master once referred to the Hindu notion
that all creation is "leela"—God's play—and
the universe is His playground. The aim of
spirituality, he claimed, is to make all life play.

This seemed too frivolous for a puritanical
visitor. "Is there no room then for work?"

"Of course there is. But work becomes spiritual
only when it is transformed into play."

Someone asked the Master what "disinterested action" meant. He replied, "Action that is loved and done for its own sake, not for any approval or profit or gain."

Then he told of a man who was hired by a researcher, taken to a backyard, and given an axe.

"Do you see that log lying there? Well I want you to go through the motions of chopping it— only you must use the reverse side of the axe, not the blade. You'll get a hundred dollars an hour for that."

The man thought the researcher was crazy, but the pay seemed excellent, so he started to work.

Two hours later he came to say, "Mister, I'm quitting."

"What's the matter? Don't you like the pay you're getting? I'll double your wages!"

"No, thank you," said the man. "The pay is fine. But when I chop wood I've got to see the chips fly!"

To a couple anxious about the upbringing of their children, the Master quoted a rabbinical saying:

"Do not limit your children to your own learning, for they have been born in another age."

"The principal reason why people are not happy
is that they get a perverse satisfaction from their
sufferings," said the Master.

He told how he was once traveling on the upper
berth of a train at night. It was impossible to
sleep because from the lower berth came the
ceaseless moan of a woman, "Oh, how thirsty
I am . . . God, how thirsty I am . . . !"

On and on went the mournful voice. The Master
finally crept down the ladder, walked through
the windy corridor of the whole length of the
train, filled two large paper cups with water,
brought them back and handed them to the
tormented woman.

"Lady, here. Water!"

"God bless you, sir. Thank you."

The Master climbed back into his berth, settled
down comfortably and was on the verge of
falling into blissful slumber when from below
came the lament, "Oh, how thirsty I *was* . . .
God, how thirsty I *was* . . . !"

A social worker poured out her woes to the Master. How much good she would be able to do for the poor if she did not have to spend so much time and energy protecting herself and her work from slander and misunderstandings.

The Master listened attentively, then responded in a single sentence: "No one throws stones at barren trees."

"Could action lead to Enlightenment?" the Master was asked.

"Only action leads to Enlightenment," was his reply, "but it must be non-profit action, done for its own sake."

He explained how he once sat in the stands with the little son of a soccer star who was playing a practice game. When the man shot a brilliant goal, everyone cheered. The kid wasn't impressed; he just sat there looking bored.

"What's the matter with you?" said the Master. "Didn't you see your father score that goal?"

"Yeah, he scored it all right—today, Tuesday. The match is on Friday—that's when the goals are needed."

The Master concluded, "Actions are valued if they help you score goals—not for themselves, alas."

The Master wasn't given to practices of devotion.

When questioned about it, he said:

"A lamp loses its rays when set beside the sun; even the tallest temple looks so tiny at the foot of a Himalayan mountain."

"My temple priest tells me that the temple is the only place for me to worship in. What do you say?"

"Your temple priest isn't the best person to consult on these matters," said the Master.

"But, he's the expert, isn't he?"

In reply the Master told of an experience he had in a foreign country as he glanced through two guidebooks he had brought. His guide frowned at the guidebooks, pointed to one of them, and said, "This one very bad guidebook. Other one better."

"Why? Does this one have more information?"

The guide shook his head. "This book say give guide five dollar. That one say give guide fifty cent."

"One reason you join a religious organization is the chance it offers you to dodge religion with a clear conscience," said the Master.

And he told of a conversation he had with a disciple who had just got engaged to a traveling salesman.

"Is he good looking?" asked the Master.

"Well, he certainly wouldn't stand out in a crowd."

"Does he have money?"

"If he does, he won't spend it."

"Does he have any bad habits?"

"He certainly smokes and drinks a lot more than is good for him."

"I don't understand you. If you can't find anything good to say about him why marry him?"

"Well, he's mostly on the road and away from home. That way I have the satisfaction of being married without the burden of a husband."

The Master hardly ever spoke of spiritual topics. He was content to eat and work and play with the disciples—and join with them in conversation on a thousand different topics ranging from the political situation of the country to the latest bar-room joke.

A visitor once said, "How can the man teach you when he'd rather tell a joke than speak of God?"

Said a disciple, "There are other ways of teaching than through the use of words."

The Master loved a game of cards and once sat
through an all-night air raid totally absorbed in
playing poker with some of his disciples. When
they stopped for drinks the conversation turned
on the subject of death.

"If I were to drop down dead in the middle of
this game, what would you do?" asked the
Master.

"What would you wish us to do?"

"Two things. First: Get the body out of the way."

"And the second?"

"Deal," said the Master.

"Why did you come to the Master?"

"Because my life was going nowhere, giving me nothing."

"So where's it going now?"

"Nowhere."

"And what's it giving you now?"

"Nothing."

"So what's the difference?"

"Now I'm going nowhere because there's nowhere to go; I'm getting nothing because there's nothing to desire."

To a man who spent years studying the Law of
his religion the Master said, "It is love that is
the key to the good life, not religion or the law."

Then he told of two Sunday-school students
who were sick of religious instructions, so one
suggested they run away.

"Run away? . . . But our fathers will get hold
of us and thrash us."

"We'll hit them back."

"What? Hit your *father?* You must be out of
your mind. Have you forgotten that God
commands us to honor our father and mother?"

"True . . . O.K., you hit my father and I'll hit
yours."

The Master claimed that it made no sense at all to define oneself as Indian, Chinese, African, American, Hindu, Christian, or Moslem, for these are merely labels.

To a disciple who claimed he was Jewish first, last, and above all else, the Master said benignly, "Your conditioning is Jewish, not your identity."

"What's my identity?"

"Nothing," said the Master.

"You mean I am an emptiness and a void?" said the incredulous disciple.

"Nothing that can be labeled," said the Master.

At the Master's birthday party a disciple
somewhat pointedly refused a glass of wine.

As he moved around the room he happened to
run into the Master who gave him a wink and
whispered, "You still have some interesting
things to learn, my friend."

"What, for instance?"

"For instance, this: You could dye your prayer
rug in wine and it would still be soaked with
God."

The Master enjoined, not austerity, but
moderation. If we truly enjoyed things, he
claimed, we would be spontaneously moderate.

Asked why he was so opposed to ascetical
practices, he replied, "Because they produce
pleasure-haters who always become people-
haters—rigid and cruel."

"But lots of pleasure-lovers are rigid and cruel."

"Not so. It is not pleasure they love for they stuff
themselves with it. What they love is the
punishment they inflict on their bodies through
excessive pleasure."

The Master taught mostly in parables and
stories. Someone asked a disciple where he got
them from.

"From God," was the reply. "When God means
you to be a healer he sends you patients; when
he makes you a teacher he sends you pupils;
when he destines you to be a Master he sends
you stories."

When asked about Jesus' injunction to his
disciples to hate their parents, the Master said,
"You will rarely find a greater enemy than
a parent."

And he told how he once met a woman at the
supermarket pushing a pram with two little
boys in it.

"What cute little kids you have," said the Master.
"How old are they?"

"The doctor," said the lady, "is three and the
lawyer two."

To those disciples who were naively confident
that there was nothing they couldn't achieve if
they went at it with a will the Master would say,
"The best things in life cannot be willed into
being."

"You can will to put food in your mouth
  but you cannot will an appetite.
You can will to lie in bed
  but you cannot will sleep.
You can will to pay someone a compliment
  but you cannot will admiration.
You can will to tell a secret
  but you cannot will trust.
You can will an act of service
  but you cannot will love."

"Each time you seek to change another," said the Master, "ask yourself this: 'What will be served by this change—my pride, my pleasure, or my profit?' "

And he told them the following story:

A man was about to jump off a bridge when a policeman rushed up to him, "No, no!" he cried, "Please don't do it. Why would a young fellow like you who hasn't even lived think of jumping into the water?"

"Because I'm sick of life."

"Now listen to me, please. If you jump into the river, I'll have to go in after you to save you. Right? Well the water is freezing cold and I've only just recovered from a bout of double pneumonia. Do you know what that means? I will die. I have a wife and four kids. Would you want to live with a thing like that on your conscience? No, of course not. So listen to me. Be good. Repent and God will forgive you. Go back home. And in the privacy and quiet of your home, hang yourself."

Irritated by the Master's paradoxical language,
a philosopher from Europe exclaimed, "I have
heard it said that east of the Suez Canal two
contradictory statements can be simultaneously
true."

The Master enjoyed that one. "East of Suez,"
he said, "and one inch into Reality. That is why
Reality is an unintelligible mystery."

There were no clocks in the monastery. When a businessman complained about the lack of punctuality, the Master said, "Ours is a cosmic punctuality, not a business punctuality."

This made no sense to the businessman, so he added, "Everything depends on your point of view. From the viewpoint of the forest, what is the loss of a leaf? From the viewpoint of the Cosmos, what is the loss of your business schedule?"

"Why are more people not Enlightened?"

"Because it isn't Truth they seek but their convenience," said the Master.

He showed this by means of a Sufi tale:

> A man in need of money sought to sell a rough carpet in the street. The first man to whom he showed it said, "This is a coarse carpet and very worn." And he bought it very cheaply.
>
> A minute later the buyer said to another man who happened along, "Here is a carpet soft as silk, sir; none like it."
>
> Said a Sufi who had witnessed the scene, "Please, carpetman, put me into your magic box that can turn a rough carpet into a smooth one, pebble into a precious stone."

"The magic box, of course," added the Master, "is called self-interest: the most effective tool in the world for turning truth into deception."

"I thought that spirituality has nothing to do with politics," said a somewhat shocked disciple when she first became acquainted with the Master's political activities.

"That's because you have no idea what spirituality is all about," was the Master's reply.

Another day he called out to her and said, "You have no idea what politics is all about either."

"Is there such a thing as selfless love?" someone asked.

In reply the master said:

> Mr. Dogood stood anxiously by as the angels in heaven examined his records. Finally the recording angel looked up and exclaimed, "But this is fabulous. This is unheard of! In your entire life you haven't committed even one tiny little sin . . . not so much as a single little peccadillo in a whole lifetime! All you did were acts of charity. Now under what category can we let you into heaven? Not as an angel because an angel you are not. Not as a human being because you haven't a single weakness. So we're going to send you back to earth for a day so that you can commit at least one sin—and come back to us a human being!"

> Poor sinless Mr. Dogood found himself back at the street corner of his hometown, unhappy and bewildered, determined to stray at least one little step from the straight and narrow. An hour passed, then two, then three and still Mr. Dogood stood there

helplessly wondering just what he
ought to do. So when a solidly built
woman gave him a wink he responded
with alacrity. The lady was far from
young or pretty—but she was his
passport to heaven, so he went off with
her for the night. When day dawned
Mr. Dogood glanced at his watch. He
must hurry. Half an hour more and he
would be carried off to heaven again.
As he was putting his clothes on he
suddenly froze, for the old lady called
out from bed, "Oh, dear, dear Mr.
Dogood, what a great act of charity
you have done tonight!"

An art writer was giving a lecture at the monastery.

"Art is found in a museum," he said, "but beauty is found everywhere, in the air, on the ground, all over the place, free for the taking—with no name attached to it."

"Exactly like spirituality," said the Master the following day when he was alone with his disciples. "Its symbols are found in the museum called a temple, but its substance is everywhere, free for the taking, unrecognized, with no name attached to it."

The Master, fascinated as he was by modern technology, refused to call it progress.

True progress for him, was "heart progress," "happiness progress," not "brain progress" or "gadget progress."

"What do you think of modern civilization?" he was once asked by a reporter.

"I think that would be a very good idea," was his reply.

When talk of Modern Progress came up one
day the Master told of two visitors from a
developing country.

He asked about the economic state of their
people. One of the callers took offense. "But
man," he said, "we're civilized; we even have
a couple of ammunition factories!"

To a social worker the Master said, "I fear you are doing more harm than good."

"Why?"

"Because you stress only one of the two imperatives of justice."

"Namely?"

"The poor have a right to bread."

"What's the other one?"

"The poor have a right to beauty."

The Master's complaint against most social activists was this: what they sought was reform, not revolution.

"There was once a very wise and gentle king," he said, "who learned that there were a number of innocent persons in his state prison. So he decreed that another, more comfortable prison be constructed for the innocent."

A disciple, in his reverence for the Master, looked upon him as God incarnate.

"Tell me, O Master," he said, "why you have come to this world."

"To teach fools like you to stop wasting their time worshiping Masters," was the answer he got.

When someone boasted of the economic and
cultural achievements of his country the Master
was quite unimpressed. "Have all those
achievements made the slightest change in the
hearts of your countrymen?" he asked.

And he told of the white man who was captured
by cannibals and brought before the chief prior
to being roasted alive. Imagine his astonishment
when he heard the chieftain speak with a perfect
Harvard accent.

"Did your years in Harvard do nothing to change
you?" asked the white man.

"Of course they did. They civilized me. After
you're roasted I shall dress for dinner and eat
you with knife and fork."

"This is your error, that you seek God outside of you," said the Master.

"Shall I then seek him inside?"

"Do you not see that your 'inside' is outside of you?" said the Master.

The Master kept constantly reminding people
of their robot-like existence: "How can you call
yourself human if every one of your thoughts,
feelings, and actions are mechanical, arising,
not from yourself but your conditioning?"

"Can anything break the conditioning and set us
free?" the disciples asked.

"Yes, awareness."

Then after a moment's thought he added, "And
catastrophe."

"Catastrophe?"

"Yes. A very English Englishman once told me
that after being shipwrecked in midocean and
swimming with another Englishman for a whole
hour, he finally succeeded in breaking loose
from his conditioning and spoke without being
introduced!"

"What did he say?"

"He said: 'Pardon me for speaking to you like
this without being introduced, but is this the
way to Southampton?' "

The Master persistently warned against the attempt to encompass Reality in a concept or a name.

A scholar in mysticism once asked, "When you speak of BEING, sir, is it eternal, transcendent being you speak of, or transcient, contingent being?"

The Master closed his eyes in thought. Then he opened them, put on his most disarming expression and said, "Yes!"

Later he said, "As soon as you put a name to Reality it ceases to be Reality."

"Even when you call it 'Reality?' " asked a mischievous disciple.

"Precisely, even when you call it 'it.' "

The Master made it his task to systematically
destroy every doctrine, every belief, every
concept of the divine, for these things, which
were originally intended as pointers, were now
being taken as descriptions.

He loved to quote the Eastern saying:

"When the sage points to the moon, all that the
idiot sees is the finger."

The Master argued with no one for he knew that what the "arguer" sought was confirmation of his beliefs, not the Truth.

He once showed them the value of an argument:

"Does a slice of bread fall with the buttered side up or down?"

"With the buttered side down, of course."

"No, with the buttered side up."

"Let's put it to the test."

So a slice of bread was buttered and thrown up in the air. It fell—buttered side up!

"I win!"

"Only because I made a mistake,"

"What mistake?"

"I obviously buttered the wrong side."

"A religious belief," said the Master, "is not a statement of Reality, but a hint, a clue about something that is a mystery, beyond the grasp of human thought. In short, a religious belief is only a finger pointing to the moon.

"Some religious people never get beyond the study of the finger.

"Others are engaged in sucking it.

"Others yet use the finger to gouge their eyes out. These are the bigots whom religion has made blind.

"Rare indeed is the religionist who is sufficiently detached from the finger to see what it is indicating—these are those who, having gone beyond belief, are taken for blasphemers."

One night the Master led his disciples into the open fields and a star-studded sky. Then, pointing toward the stars, he looked at the disciples and said, "Now concentrate on my finger, everyone."

They got the point.

Alarmed at the Master's tendency to destroy every statement of belief in God one disciple cried out, "I'm left with nothing to hold on to."

"That's what the fledgling says when pushed out of its nest!" said the Master.

Later he said, "Do you expect to fly when you are securely settled in the nest of your beliefs? That isn't flying. That's flapping your wings!"

"Humility is not silly self-deprecation," said the Master. "It comes from understanding that all you succeed in doing by your efforts is change your behavior—not yourself."

"So true change is effortless?"

"That's right," said the Master.

"And how does it come about?"

"Through awareness," said the Master.

"And what does one do to become aware?"

"What does one do, when one is asleep, to wake from sleep?" said the Master.

"So there is no true good that one can take pride in?"

In reply, the Master told of a conversation he overheard:

> "Our Master—what a voice he has, how divinely he chants!"

> "Huh! If I had his voice I'd chant just as well!"

When the ruler of a neighboring kingdom announced his intention of visiting the monastery everyone was excited. Only the Master was his usual self.

The King was ushered into the presence of the Master; he bowed low in greeting and said, "It is my belief that you have attained to mystical perfection so I have come to ask about the essence of the mystical."

"Why?" said the Master.

"It is my wish to inquire into the nature of being so as to be able to control my own being and that of my subjects and bring my nation into harmony."

"Good," said the Master, "but I must warn you that when you have gone far enough in your inquiry you will discover that the harmony you seek is achieved not through control but through surrender."

Said the self-righteous preacher, "What, in your judgment, is the greatest sin in the world?"

"That of the person who sees other human beings as sinners," said the Master.

"There are, indeed, two types of human beings: the pharisees and the publicans," said the Master after reading the parable of Jesus.

"How does one recognize the pharisees?"

"Simple. They are the ones who do the classifying!" said the Master.

"All human beings are about equally good or bad," said the Master who hated to use those labels.

"How can you put a saint on an equal footing with a sinner?" protested a disciple.

"Because everyone is the same distance from the sun. Does it really lessen the distance if you live on top of a skyscraper?"

The Master maintained that what the whole
world held to be true is false; so the pioneer
is always in a minority of one. He said:

"You think of Truth as if it were a formula that
you can pick up from a book. Truth is
purchased at the price of loneliness. If you wish
to follow Truth you must learn to walk alone."

"I am ready to go anywhere in search of Truth," proclaimed the ardent disciple.

The Master was amused. "When are you going to set out?" he asked.

"The moment you tell me where to go."

"I suggest you travel in the direction your nose is pointing in."

"Yes. But where do I stop?"

"Anywhere you wish."

"And will the Truth be there?"

"Yes. Right in front of your nose, staring your unseeing eyes in the face."

"Is Enlightenment easy or difficult?"

"It is as easy and as difficult as seeing what is right before your eyes."

"How can seeing what is right before one's eyes be difficult?"

To that the Master responded with the following anecdote:

> A girl greeted her boyfriend with: "Notice anything different about me?"
>
> "New dress?"
>
> "No."
>
> "New shoes?"
>
> "No. Something else."
>
> "I give up."
>
> "I'm wearing a gas mask."

The disciple was a Buddhist. "What is the mind of Buddha?" he asked.

"Why not ask about your own mind or self instead of someone else's?" said the Master.

"Then, what is my self, O Master?"

"For that you have to learn what is known as 'the secret act.'"

"What is the secret act?"

"This," said the Master, as he closed his eyes and opened them.

The Master explained to his disciples that Enlightenment would come if they achieved non-interpretative looking.

What, they wanted to know, was interpretative looking.

This is how the Master explained it:

> A couple of Catholic laborers were hard at work on the road in front of a brothel when they saw a rabbi slink into the house of ill repute.
>
> "Well, what can you expect?" they said to each other.
>
> After a while a parson slipped in. No surprise. "What can you expect?"
>
> Then comes the local Catholic priest who covers his face with a cloak just before he dives into the building. "Now isn't that dreadful? One of the girls must have taken ill."

A disciple once asked the Master how he could enter the Path.

"Do you hear the murmur of that stream as it passes by the monastery?"

"Yes."

"That is an excellent way to enter the Path."

The Master loved to tell this one about himself:

After his first child was born he went to the nursery and saw his wife standing over the baby's crib. Silently he watched her as she gazed at the sleeping infant. In her face he saw wonder, incredulity, rapture, ecstasy. Moved to tears, he tiptoed over to her, put an arm round her waist and whispered, "I know exactly what you must feel, my dear."

Startled into consciousness his wife blurted out, "Yes. For the life of me I don't see how they can make a crib like that for twenty bucks."

Any time the topic of God came up the Master would insist that God is essentially beyond the grasp of human thought—a Mystery—and so anything said about God was true, not of Him, but of our concept of Him.

The disciples never really grasped at the implications of this till the Master one day undertook to show them.

"It is not true to say that God created the world or God loves us or God is great—for of God nothing may be said. So, in the interest of accuracy one should say: Our God-concept created the world, Our God-concept loves us, Our God-concept is great."

"If that is true, should we not drop every concept we have of the divine?"

"There would be no need to abandon your idols if you did not construct them in the first place," said the Master.

It bothered some of the disciples that the Master seemed to care so little whether people believed in a personal God or not.

He once quoted to them a sentence that was to become a favorite with him. It was from the diary of U.N. Secretary General Dag Hammarskjöld:

"God does not die on the day we cease to believe in a personal deity, but we die on the day when our lives cease to be illumined by the steady radiance, renewed daily, of a *wonder,* the source of which is beyond all reason."*

*Markings. New York: Alfred A. Knopf, 1965.

The Master once saw a large crowd assembled at the monastery gate singing hymns "at" him and holding up a banner that read: CHRIST IS THE ANSWER.

He walked over to the dour-looking man who held the sign and said, "Yes, but what is the question?"

The man was momentarily taken aback, but recovered quickly enough to say, "Christ is not the answer to a question, but the answer to our problems."

"In that case, what is the problem?"

Later he said to the disciples, "If Christ is, indeed, the answer, then this is what Christ means: the clear understanding of *who* is creating the problem, and how."

"What can I do to attain Enlightenment?" asked
the eager disciple.

"See Reality as it is," said the Master.

"Well, what can I do to see Reality as it is?"

The Master smiled and said, "I have good news
and bad news for you, my friend."

"What's the bad news?"

"There's nothing you can do to see—
it's a gift."

"And what's the good news?"

"There's nothing you can do to see—
it's a gift."

Human problems stubbornly resist ideological solutions as the labor reformer found to his dismay when he took the Master to watch a trench being dug with modern methods. "This machine," he said, "has taken jobs from scores of men. They ought to destroy it and put a hundred men with shovels in that ditch."

"Yes," said the Master. "Or better still, a thousand men with teaspoons."

The preacher was determined to extract an unambiguous declaration of belief in God from the Master.

"Do you believe there is a God?"

"Of course, I do," said the Master.

"And He made everything. Do you believe that?"

"Yes, yes," said the Master. "I certainly do."

"And who made God?"

"You," said the Master.

The preacher was aghast. "Do you seriously mean to tell me that it is I who made God?"

"The one you are forever *thinking* about and *talking* about—yes!" said the Master placidly.

The Master dismissed ideologues for the simple reason that their theories sounded reasonable but would never fit Reality.

He told of an ideologue who said, "This is a crazy world. The rich buy on credit though they have plenty of money but the poor, who are penniless, must pay cash."

"So what do you suggest?" someone asked.

"Turn things around. Make the rich pay cash and give the poor credit."

"But if a shopkeeper gives credit to the poor, he'll end up poor himself."

"Great!" said the ideologue, "Then he can buy on credit too!"

The Master found it tiresome to speak with
people who were forever bent on defending
the existence of God or discussing His nature
while they neglected the all-important task of
self-awareness, which alone could bring them
love and liberation.

To a group of people who asked him to speak to
them of God, he said, "What you seek, alas, is
to talk of God rather than see Him; and you see
Him as you *think* he is, not as he *actually* is. For
God is manifest, He is not hidden. Why talk?
Open you eyes and see."

Later he added, "Seeing is the easiest thing in
the world. All you need to do is raise the
shutters of your God-thoughts."

Said a disciple, "We have to dress and eat—
how do we get out of all that?"

"We eat. We dress," said the Master.

"I do not understand."

"If you don't understand, get dressed and eat
your food."

Later he said, "You never rise above anything
you avoid facing."

Later still, "People who want to rise above a
well-cooked meal and a well-tailored garment,
are out of their spiritual minds."

The most common cause of unhappiness, the Master claimed, is the decision people make to be unhappy. That is why of two persons who find themselves in exactly the same situation one is happy, the other miserable.

He told how his little daughter had been reluctant to go to summer camp. In an attempt to ease her misgivings, the Master addressed several postcards to himself and gave them to the child.

"Now every day," he said, "just write 'I'm fine,' on one of these cards and drop it in the mailbox."

The girl pondered this and asked, "How do you spell 'miserable'?"

The Master was a great supporter of historical research. His one complaint about history students, however, was that they generally passed over the most valuable lessons that history has to offer.

"For instance?" asked one student.

"For instance, the sight of problems, once so vital, but now no more than cold abstractions in a book. The characters in history's drama, once thought to be so mighty, but in reality mere puppets pulled by strings so obvious to us, so pathetically unsuspected by them!"

Said the Master, "What you call a friendship is really a business deal: Live up to my expectations, give me what I want and I shall love you; refuse me and my love sours into resentment and indifference."

He told of the man who came home to his wife and his cute little three-year-old daughter at the end of a hard day at the office.

"Have you a kiss for Daddy?"

"No."

"I'm ashamed of you. Your Daddy works hard all day to bring home a little money, and this is how you behave! Come on now, where's the kiss?"

Looking him in the eye, the cute little three-year-old said, "Where's the money?"

Said one disciple, "I don't trade my love for money."

Said the Master, "Isn't it as bad—or worse—that you trade it for love?"

"What does it mean to be Enlightened?"

"To see."

"What?"

"The hollowness of success, the emptiness of achievements, the nothingness of human striving," said the Master.

The disciple was appalled. "But isn't that pessimism and despair?"

"No. That's the excitement and freedom of the eagle gliding over a bottomless ravine."

A despondent disciple complained that, because of his handicaps, he was being cheated by life.

"Cheated?" cried the Master. "Cheated? Look around you man! With every moment of consciousness you are being grossly overpaid!"

The Master followed that up with the story of the hotel owner who complained bitterly about the effect on his business of a new highway the government had built.

"Look," said a friend. "I just don't understand you. I see a NO VACANCY sign each night in front of your hotel."

"You can't go by that. Before they built the highway I used to turn away thirty or forty people each day. Now I never turn away more than twenty-five."

Added the Master, "When you are determined to feel bad, even non-existent customers are real."

That reminded the disciples of the pessimist
who said, "Life is so awful, it would have been
better not to have been born."

"Yes," replied the Master, with a twinkle in his
eye, "but how many have that kind of luck?
One in ten thousand maybe."

The Master must have known that his words were frequently beyond his disciples' comprehension. He spoke them nonetheless in the knowledge that a day would surely come when they would take root and blossom in the hearts that heard him.

One day he said:

"Time always seems so long when you *wait*— for a vacation, an examination, for something yearned for or dreaded in the future.

"But to those who dare to surrender to the experience of the present moment—with no thought about the experience, no desire that it return or be avoided—time is transformed into the radiance of Eternity."

"You are destroyed by life's tranquillity," said the Master to an easy-going disciple. "Only disaster can save you."

And this is how he explained it:

"Throw a frog into a pan of boiling water and it will jump out in a second. Place it in a pan of water that is heated very gradually and it will lose the tension to spring when the moment to leap arrives."

Said the governor, "Is there any advice you can give me in the exercise of my office?"

"Yes. Learn how to give orders."

"How?"

"So that others can receive them without feeling inferior," said the Master.

When asked how one discovered Silence the
Master told this story:

> A factory was interested in buying
> bullfrog skins. A farmer wired the
> company that he could supply any
> quantity up to a hundred thousand and
> more on demand. The company wired
> back: "Send first consignment fifty
> thousand."
>
> Two weeks later one single pathetic
> frog skin came through the mail with
> this note: "Sirs: I apologize. This is
> all the frog skins there were in the
> neighborhood. The noise certainly
> fooled me."

Later the Master said, "Investigate the noise
that people make. Then see through the noise
that you yourself are making and you will find
nothing, emptiness—and Silence."

"My life is like shattered glass," said the visitor. "My soul is tainted with evil. Is there any hope for me?"

"Yes," said the Master. "There is something whereby each broken thing is bound again and every stain made clean."

"What?"

"Forgiveness."

"Whom do I forgive?"

"Everyone:
Life,
God,
your neighbor
—especially yourself."

"How is that done?"

"By understanding that no one is to blame," said the Master. "NO ONE."

It scandalized people to hear the Master say that true religion was not a social matter. He said:

There was a little polar bear who asked his mother, "Mother, was my daddy also a polar bear?"

"Of course he was a polar bear."

After a while, "Tell me, mommy, was my grandfather also a polar bear?"

"Yes, he was also a polar bear."

"What about my great-grandfather? Was he a polar bear too?"

"Yes, he was. Why are you asking?"

"Because I'm freezing."

The Master concluded: "Religion is neither social nor inherited. It is an intensely personal thing."

"I seek the meaning of existence," said the stranger.

"You are, of course, assuming," said the Master, "that existence has a meaning."

"Doesn't it?"

"When you experience existence as it is—not as you *think* it is—you will discover that your question has no meaning," said the Master.

"Isn't there such a thing as social liberation?"

"Of course there is," said the Master.

"How would you describe it?"

"Liberation from the need to belong to the herd," said the Master.

"My friend," said the Master to the freedom fighter in his prison cell, "you will face your execution valiantly tomorrow. Only one thing holds you back from meeting death with joy."

"What is it?"

"The wish that your exploits be remembered. The desire that future generations applaud your heroic deeds."

"Is there anything wrong with that?" asked the condemned man.

"Has it ever struck you that if posterity remembers, it is not you that your actions will be attached to but your NAME?"

"Aren't the two things the same?"

"Ah no, my friend! Your name is the sound you respond to. Your label. Who are YOU?"

That was all the man needed to "die" that very night—even before the firing squad came for him at dawn.

Word of the Master's conversation with the executed man leaked out to the disciples.

"Surely one's name is something more than a sound," they said.

In response the Master told them about the street vendor who became a multimillionaire, only, instead of his signature on a check, he would mark checks with two crosses because he was illiterate.

One day the banker was surprised to see three crosses on a check. "It's my wife," said the millionaire by way of explanation, "she has social ambitions. The second X in the row is my middle name."

The disciples were sitting on a bank of a river.

"If I fall off this bank will I drown?" one of them asked.

"No," said the Master. "It isn't falling in that causes you to drown; it's staying in."

When commenting on Jesus' image of persons
who strained at gnats and swallowed camels,
the Master explained how once, during the war,
he herded everyone into the monastery
basement during a vicious air raid. All day they
sat there while bombs fell around them. When
evening came two of the men could take it no
longer. "We've had enough," they said. "Bombs
or no bombs, we're going home."

They walked away—and were back in the
basement three minutes later.

"I see you've changed your minds," said the
Master with a smile.

"Yes," they said, annoyed, "it's started to rain."

"How joyful the Master seems," a visitor remarked.

Said a disciple, "One always treads with a joyful step when one has dropped the burden called the ego."

The Master was asked what he thought of the achievements of modern technology. This was his reply:

An absent-minded professor was late for his lecture. He jumped into a cab and shouted, "Hurry! At top speed!"

As the cab sped along he realized he hadn't told the driver where to go, so he shouted, "Do you know where I want to go?"

"No, sir," said the cabbie, "but I'm driving as fast as I can."

A large crowd of friends and former disciples gathered to celebrate the Master's ninetieth birthday.

Before the party was over the Master rose to speak:

"Life," he said, "is measured by the quality not by the numbers of one's days."

When a mammoth meeting was called to protest against the government's manufacture of nuclear bombs the Master and his disciples were conspicuous in the crowd.

Loud applause greeted the statement, "Bombs kill people!" The Master shook his head and muttered, "That isn't true. *People* kill people!"

When he realized he had been overheard by the man standing next to him, he leaned over and said, "Well, I'll correct that: *ideas* kill people."